The Bunker Book

Anne Babson

For information contact:
Unsolicited Press
Portland, Oregon
www.unsolicitedpress.com
orders@unsolicitedpress.com
619-354-8005

Cover Design: Kathryn Gerhardt
Editor: Bekah Stogner

ISBN: 978-1-956692-44-0

I forever stand on the shoulders of giants—among those are Marilyn Hacker, Allan Gurganus, Cornelius Eady, and the Late Thomas Lux, Frank McCourt and Jane Cooper—all of whom taught me to write, or at least write better.

I now inhabit a world of encouragers and peers in the writing world—I am grateful for the encouragement from the writers of the Peauxdunque Writers Alliance, a New Orleans Krewe of Writers who drink and laugh together while engaging in the serious work of revision.

I am grateful to my husband, who supports me in my efforts in general.

To YH.

TABLE OF CONTENTS

"You want the...least problematic shelter, and that is why...if you are interested in learning more about the underground bunkers... see this page."
—Web copy from Rising S Company: We don't sell fear. We sell preparedness.

"We have come to console you in your anguish and perplexity, dear friend, and explain the things that trouble your soul and confuse your thoughts."
—Christine de Pizan, *The Book of the City of Ladies*, Ineke Hardy, Tr.

"And though my...comfort...may be of little avail to the needy...who will deny that it should be given for all that it may be worth to gentle ladies much rather than to men?"
—Boccacio, Decameron, Proem 8-9, J.M. Rigg, Tr.

BIENVENUE AU BUNKER

My library, a block of volumes stonewalling
Me inside my head, form my true calling.
    I endure endless war and sometime plague
    Here, sipping philosophers' ideas too vague
    To really poison me, unlike unboiled water,
    Which I avoid. On oceans of *bons mots,* otter-
    Like, I float above swells, cracking nuts, taking notes.
    I hear distant guns fire, or are those anecdotes

Tweeting through seams in my palatial barricade
Here where I hole myself up from fusillades?
    It's too perilous to stray beyond the bookshelves.
    Others pound the ark in the rain. We save ourselves.
    Here, prefect bound perfectly, the dead resurrect,
    Speak volumes, tell me to gather *pensées,* erect

A city safe for women built on heroic
Couplets. Clearly, this makes much more sense than epics
    Unfolding outside this bespoke, book-lined bunker.
    Unabashed Kardashians roam while I hunker
    Here! I judge films by canisters, books by covers.
    Each cell, each page I scan promises new lovers.

Derrida tells me *Il n'y a pas de hors texte,*
But I bury myself here to avoid what comes next.

BLOOD OR MILK

"The symbols of collective security are being used to build collective
aggression.
[Would we enter a] century of blood or milk?"

—*Henry Wallace*

Blood or milk—
    Those are the choices
    For the flow.
No one can stand in a river while it
    Clots between his toes,
    Curdles against his lips
The same way twice.

Blood or milk—
    Those are the choices
    For the stains
Spilling over the countertop
    Into our babies' laps,
    Spattering the sidewalk
At the edge of the church parking lot.

Blood or milk—
    Those are the choices.

Together, they are not Kosher,
      The juicy rose flesh of the suckling
      And the thinning milk of its mother.
      Together, they are unfit food for Massai
      Leaping heavenward from the plains.

Blood or milk—
      The September moon hangs full
Like the white of an eye turned yet higher
      Or, in the red dust of the bitter harvest,
      An accusing glare.
Those are the choices.

THE CITY WITH GHOSTS

"They want to increase tourism by filling the city with ghosts."
                                    —Maurice Carlos Ruffin

Ignoring doctors' warnings, businessmen make big boasts.
To increase tourism, they fill the city with ghosts.

The slave market then is now our finest hotel.
Visit its bar. Sazeracs swill the city with ghosts.

First a roustabout, then a rough neck, he came upstream
For grunt work after they oil-spilled the city with ghosts.

Gothic novels stack behind every shutter. We don't
Bury the dead—no room. Books thrill the city with ghosts.

A runaway from Podunk, she hitched rides, blew truckers.
She thought she would make her way—until the city with ghosts.

We lurk behind curtains. Some of us catch new lovers.
Perfect strangers Netflix-and-chill the city with ghosts.

"Can't you see that there is nothing to see here? You have
Imagined all the deaths!" They shill the city with ghosts.

After Katrina, moving to Beaumont, they both tried
To forget. Their thoughts wander still the city with ghosts

"Death is expensive, Miss Stella!" Shouted the tourists.
Their conference canceled, they bill the city with ghosts.

We dance away from funerals, for the dead abide
Here always. Our last rites instill the city with ghosts.

The ones who want parades now say heat kills the virus,
But July ferments and grills the city with ghosts.

Babsons survive plagues, and thus will I. I kill some rats.
I kill roaches. No one can kill the city with ghosts.

JUNE BUNKER

People save top tiers of wedding cakes in freezers.
Miss Havisham petrifies hers. Jane Austen leads
Her readers to the altar, then strands them all there.
Rick's last free train leaves without his Ilsa.

So-called friends, save Lisa, knew he cheated.
They didn't say boo. When I demanded of him,
"Come on! We have to resist these motherfuckers!
They are burning books in the school yards!" And he
made

Sardonic remarks about a functionally
Illiterate America. They knew he would
Never join me in my curfew-breaking sorties.
They knew when I said, *"Words mean something!"* he wouldn't

Even drive U-Hauls to the grain elevator
That descended the abandoned missile silo.
They knew he wouldn't unload boxes I labeled
"BIOHAZARD" filled with libraries and supplies.

They knew. Only my rescue pit-bull called shotgun.
Miss Havisham sits in the drawing room, clock-stopped
By her author, stuck in her bitterness. Not I.
I just wait it out. He never asked that last night

> Where I was going. He knew. There is a timer
> On the pressure lock. I have enough to survive
> The decade if I need to. My dog and I hope
> For parole. The books down here could last an epoch.

I will take myself out of the freezer and share myself once more.
I am coming soon with alpha through omega, *Beowulf* through
  Angela's Ashes.
I will share these living words, the priest bearing a eucharist
To be taken by the faithful, or at least by those who repent.

POEM IN WHICH I AM A MEDIEVAL CODEX

Flip through me. You'll see who
  I am.
My provenance is unconfirmed, confusing,
    But the scribal intervention is unmistakable.

  I am
  A *florilegium*—
The kind noblemen kept for plague seasons like this one, snippets
from diverse sources,
    Endings changed to keep the reader happy while the
    people outside die.
      A book for storm drinking reading before the
      power goes out again.

  I am

  The archive marked "*raptus*," the London docket, circa
  1350,
All sobbing scraped off parchment by a bitter,
    Celibate man in cell, monk's cell. Today, he buys an
    AK-47 in Kenner, follows Stormy Daniels on Twitter.

I am

Middle French scrawled

instruction —How to clean hunting Falcon guts when one of

yours eats rotten meat—White

Flour gruel the cure—

Then give it two glasses of milk punch from the slow-
spinning

Carousel Bar after closing time. That way,

Tourists won't post the winding gyre to

Instagram.

I am

A rhyming Middle English charm parchment.

A woman places me on her pregnant belly while she prays.

Flip me over. Make me a pelvis tent.

Petition Saint Raymond Nonnatus, patron of labor.

Then get a good midwife.

I don't know about birthing babies. I just said I did to
impress the white

Doctor. Scarlett slaps me. Violins swell.

I am

Another version of Petrarch's and Chaucer's

Griselda, psychologically tortured by her husband—

Only in this version, she slits his throat, holds his liver in a basket
in the market square.

Nobody chases her with pitchforks as she slinks uphill to the
        Ursulines Convent,
        But a jazz quartet—
        The Four Horsemen—follow her,
        Playing
        "I'll Fly Away."

        I am
        A Latin hagiography of Saint Joan, one where she
survives the
Stake.
        Angel voices tell her to ride off to
        Algiers and leave the
        French dukes to duke it out until the
        Feast of Epiphany.

                I am
        An illuminated topless
Eleanor of Aquitaine on
        Crusade down
        Bourbon Street. I list the recipe for
        Sazeracs in medical
        Latin.
        Selah.

I am

A Latin canticle without notation—

A mash-up of "*Exultávit Spíritus Meus*" and a club mix of
Saint Vincent. Sick beats, plague beats, syncopate, then
interrupt.

I am

The Early Dutch County of Loon Beguine House
Monastic Rule.

None of the women who pray there are saintly—only uppity.
The church tries the women for heresy.
Spoiler alert: the
Rule ends with this
Middle French mystery:
Laissez les bons temps rouler.

I am

Julian of Norwich transcribed by the Friends of the Holy
Spirit.

I crawl out of the anchorite cell *ex cathedra* before dawn
To gather hazelnuts in
September, to hold them in the small of my hand the
way that
God holds the whole world.
I sneak back before matins.
I sneak out again the next summer.

I wander through a sugar cane field in
South Louisiana.
Confronted at eye level
By an enormous spider swinging on white
Web threads between two long, green stalks, I understand
the omen.
I run back to Norwich.
I wall myself up again. I should have stayed on my knees on the
stone floor!
I catch the disease. I cough on my death bed.
Before I flatline,
My bed morphs into the kidney-shaped pool at
Graceland, fills with
Blood gushing from the
Crucifix.
Elvis and I backstroke.
"Arte thou wele paide that I sufferde for thee?"
The Crucified
Asks, laughing.
I smile, hold the hazelnut up to him — a sponge dipped
in vinegar.
"All will be well," I say, *"and all manner of thing will be well,"*
I reply, but then,
I check my phone.

ALTARPIECE DYPTICH

I.

Horses bite. I extend my
Child palm flat, green apple slices
Perching in it. Mammoth velvet
lips mumble against my fingers.

I squeal. The old horses, nonplussed,
Continue to nibble my gifts.
I look at my nanny, who brought
Me into this unfenced meadow,

And I squeal again. She offers
Sugar cubes out of a plastic
Bag. My bare hand turns plate again.
The giant tongue rasps against me.

II.

A penitent these days, I kneel.
I smell wax, mildew, and incense.
High heels echo against worn tiles.
My meadow lives within me now,

Hidden in middle-aged *corpus*.
The monks chant behind wood shutters.
I stand. I sit. I stand. I sit.
The monks mutter "*gloria*."

The sugar burns within me now.
The apple rots and sprouts its seeds.
The nanny left. The girl grew up.
Sacristans light those old votives.

Stones serve as exoskeleton.
The wafer waits on my flat palm.
Anchoress interred between walls,
I worship legally deceased.

THE LETTER THORN

On *The Lyndsfarne Gospels*, stuck like a tethered thorn
Through the Old English parchment, preens the letter thorn.

Her pains multiplied. They bloated fecund. She felt guilt
Triplet, quintuplet sorrow, octuplet her thorn.

After momma's burial—the casino! They
Gambled her grave flowers, even bet her thorn.

Today, if a man wants to win big, he fights for
First blood, breaking rivals' skin with his go-getter thorn.

The sportsman snags in the swamp with a brambled pole,
Snaring mud fish and stone fish with his netter thorn.

He was competitive about everything!
On his crucifix head, he claimed a better thorn.

It doesn't make sense any more to garden, she thought,
If watering a rose requires a wetter thorn.

Old English, meet this new American woman.
Runes from her berry bushes, Anne has met her thorn.

AUGUST BUNKER

"There is a river, the streams whereof shall
make glad the city of God, the holy
place of tabernacles of the Most High."

—Ps. 46:4

Jerusalem bakes in a hot desert.
An underground stream just got discovered
By people digging a railroad tunnel.
Under the Sisters of Zion Convent,
They discovered a natural pool, not
Kidney-shaped, like the blue pool at Graceland.
In God's city, the river runs under.
This tabernacle of my texts gets cooled
By the Mississippi. Is God's heart glad?
I lift its gilded cover, flip heavy
Pages, and look up my circumstances.

I read "therefore will not we fear, though the
Earth be removed, and though the mountains be
Carried into the midst of the sea; the
Waters thereof roar troubled, the mountains
Shake with the swelling thereof. Selah."
I shut the book.

I look down the poplar shelves.
I walk to the wall.
 I lean my ear to
The concrete.
I hear gurgling.
Selah.

RIVER CANTO

I wish I could promise you that I were not wrong;
The icebergs melt in this river's global warming.
The humidity cooks the world. It won't be long.

The lido deck's *chanteuse*, *décolletée*, sings her song.
She is tone deaf, if svelte, her lyrics alarming.
I wish I could promise you that I were not wrong.

This bâteau mouche's cantos are Piaf's fête's flons flons.
The sea level rises? Begin plankton farming!
The humidity cooks the world. It won't be long.

The barman pours cocktails with water from a bong.
The hammock swing of waves is fatally charming.
I wish I could tell you that I were not wrong.

I extricate my thoughts with a pair of ice tongs.
They are slippery, melting, shrinking, unforming.
The humidity cooks the world. It won't be long.

How can the feeble age preach sermons to the strong?
My daughter, it is yourself you should be arming.
I wish I could tell you that I were not wrong.
The humidity cooks the world. It won't be long.

NORSE EXPLORERS REACH THE MISSISSIPPI

I.

Whorled—like the son who becomes
The dragon— the spine dips
Like a Side- Winding stream,
Beowulf's Gaets (by Lief
Eriksson of other ships)
Arrive at last at the river's lips.

After the Vineland which they vanquished,
They trek inland looking for gold.

They see it snaking darkly
Like the tail of the lovely she-
Demon who bargained death
Against glory for go-getters.

They, too, have   thorn-lettered

Their names to   the contract

Their laird signed.   They, too,

Could own an   open landscape

Peppered by   people to vanquish

In *weltschmerz*   and walled-up regret.

They stand on   the steep bluff

And overlook   the oval arc

Of the current.   They crave more.

Without leaving   Wattled huts,

They go home   to glaciers again.

II.

The path of this   Mississippi

Changes every year.   Floods crop up

In new places   where no one

Thought to put   paved levees.

31

After those Vikings,   Mark Twain wrote
That steamboat pilots   struck envy
In every schoolboy's   book bag, and now

I stand here.   All explorers
Have gone. Map   topographers
Use satellite.   Unclear curves
Get clarified   electronically.

III.

I crave more.   Call the she-demon —
I think she's   slot-machining
With nickel slugs   at the casino—
I'm almost ready   to write it off,
Beowolf-   style, battle-wearily.
Maybe I want   sons so badly
I'll sleep in   the snakepit.

Call her. Pour mead on the carpet—
Then, she comes. When cheap booze
Flows, when wrestlers watch football screens,
When oldies blare out speakers,
She comes. Call her carefully;
She's dressed to kill. Call her for me

To strike the pact again for stately
Favor in exchange for chasing the
Mystery Mississippi,
Amphibian skin in fog,
That I might manifest
Some heroic inclination,
Vanquishing Viking thugs in
The unlit woods of Warren County.

Call her. I'll Cock the hammer—
Think of Thor. Call her over.

I'll thorn the Parchment through.

33

APRIL BUNKER

The dog and I hear rumbling again.
I gasp, then sigh when rain staccato follows.
How many fields lay fallow above us?
Here, I flip the page to a scene of planters.
The peasants wear clogs. So do I down here.

Up there, I wonder if the bees came back.
The only buzzing here is the crackle in wires
Where the connection gets so old, it echoes.
Does anyone dig a shallow grave for grain,
Then hold a vigil for a green resurrection?

THE NEW ECONOMY

The wrinkled homeless man squatting on the milk crate
shakes his balding head and mutters. Above, black train
tracks elevated, oxidizing, creaking, wait,
gaping empty save for wild grass and rats, for pain
as we at last yank them, the final extinct teeth
in a putrid dinosaur mouth, to sweep wide, clear
the path for sterile test tube towers underneath
a sky scraped clean of view-blockers, shadows, and tear-
streaking in any rain but this time's acid rain.
We have even outgrown the El, the iron gates.
We are digital now, wireless, and we are stain-
resistant, fire-retardant. But watch how our dates
of expiration in the shiny market near!
Soon, the store stocking us will empty us in fear.

MARGERY KEMPE WEEPS ON MY SHOULDER

Monks tossed her out of church caterwauling.

She wept wailing under bleeding Jesus.

On pilgrimage, she complained about them,
The sister travelers—they were tourists.

She saw gilded saint relics and sniveled.

Via Dolorosa? Not dolorous
More than she as she stumbled through stations,
Annoying Jerusalem with her howls.

Now, Margery lies splayed down here with me,
Trapped in an old palimpsest, she cries out.

She envisions His suffering mother.

She watches government execute Him.

That is why she cries everywhere she goes.

That's why I hunker here, too, Margery.

BUNKER CUISINE

When I started looking for basements in
A city below sea-level, I found
Full-spectrum lamps where a pot dealer farmed.

    I found mildew cops left behind after
    They handcuffed him. Lamps never turned
    State's evidence against their former boss.

They just lay in the muck, but they cast light
When I said, "Let there be light" down here.
I grow parsley and watercress, basil

    And green onions. The meat is all freeze-dried.
    Sometimes, I put down the book. The pit bull
    Follows me as I harvest bunker crops.

We eat well down here. I have k-rations
But won't get scurvy. The dog catches rats.
I pilfered all this wine from Galatoire's.

    Their *cave* is so big, nobody knows
    Half of it went missing. I dug tunnels
    That way, got the best bottles. Then I plugged

Up the burrow, just in case. For water—
Do you remember when everyone's bill
From the Sewerage and Water Board

Was too high that month—computer error—
Every customer complained and sued?
I was piping cisterns to sustain me.

I don't intend to die here. I will leave,
But I can stay longer than bodies do
In the town's above-ground mausolea

Without running out of baths and dinners,
Microgreen Salads and Salisbury steaks,
Perrier Jouet And Château Lafite.

Cher lecteur, mon semblable, mon frère,
Chere lectrice, ma semblable, ma soeur,
Bon appetit, et à votre santé!

COMMANDO LYRIC 1

I am writing this on the map
To steady my trigger finger.
It shakes now. They bombarded us
Every night last week. I am
The only shooter left, the worst one
At the beginning of this mess,
But now, by default, the best. I
Remember a charcoal dirt path
I took to a grotto. The mist
And terns lifted off it slowly.
I felt peaceful there. My scope shows
Three of them now. When the fuel truck
Rolls in at sunrise, I'll fire.

BUENOS AIRES 1952

Stir your coffee, *bitte*!   That's what a tourist
Would do! Chat. Smile. Nod. Good.   I won't tell Jew-
Journalists tracking us or Wiesenthal,

But in frankness: Yes—on some sweaty nights,
I do leap up screaming dreaming of them.
They stand at the sheets' edge—   gaunt, vigilant

In stripes, tattooed arms extended lance-like
To ghost-joust me.   Yes —   I do smell ovens
In tail-pipe exhaust, in August vapors.

But I wipe my face.   In morning mirrors,
While on "holiday," I practice my smile.
                Understand, *kollege*, nobody inhales

The ashes inside our sunburnt heads!
Regrets???   I counted on better from you!
So kindish!   You crush bugs under

Your loafers today.   Back there, in Poland,
No difference—   none!   That tango music
Gives me hot headaches, not remorse!   What days!

Don't you recall our weekend picnics there?
Just us and Georg and the lady guards
On that hillside just upwind of our work?

Such fresh raspberries!   We were baronets!
I regret it ended.   Soon, they'll capture us,
Nuremberg us, yes—   but who can kill us?

What we have done, they themselves will do soon.
Perhaps they'll peter out,   tire of chasing
Philosopher knights,   inscribe "NEVER FORGET"—
But they will forget!   They think they're cured,
But we're not the plague!   We're just the buboes.
They circulate us in their own blood.

OUTLAW SAINTS

The violence you have done… will overwhelm you…For you have shed man's blood; you have destroyed lands and cities and everyone in them. Of what value is an idol, since a man has carved it?…For he who makes it trusts in his own creation; he makes idols that cannot speak.

—Habbakuk 2:17-18

Here in Juarez, we started with Saint Jude, but *coño*,
He wouldn't bless the bullets or the vengeance, right?
And vengeance is the only way—turning the cheek,
That gets you a cap in the ass, *mi padre*.

So the shrine we put up in the garage near where
We bag the shit before it goes up north in mules—
We have this whole thing going—but I can't tell you.
That confessional seal thing of yours—a racket—

And why should I trust you? You wear gang colors, too,
Son—black with the white nick in your collar; how is
That so different than the black teardrops we nick
Into our cheeks for each enemy we ice?

So we built the shrine to *Santa Muerte*, Holy
Death, like the skulls on the day of the dead we eat,

The cakes in the graveyards with our great-grandmothers,
Skull-eating was Aztec and Conquistador, too.

We didn't invent this—I mean, the genocide—
Isn't that what you call it? I read that in school
Before I quit and got me a real job right here.
Yes, I pour whiskey in front of the skeleton.

And then there's Malverde, I think *en engles* it's
"Bad Green," right? He was a thug who really lived, who
Really died, but he stole from the rich and gave to
Los olvidados, God's forgotten kids. You know,

I get it. I have me some kids, too, and I don't
See them, neither, so I don't hold no grudge, *padre*.
So I pray where it doesn't feel so forgotten.
I mean, it's rough out there. When they fire, we fire back.

I'll build you a saint, *padre*. How do you want it?
I could name it, "Holy Child Abuse Cover-Up"
Or maybe just, "Holy Ignore Them." I like that—
Your face as a model. I'll design a tattoo.

ALTARPIECE WHERE I KNEEL BEFORE THE HEAD OF JOHN THE BAPTIST

I paid for this gouache-on-wood panel, so I get to photobomb it.
Behind the Apostles and the local patron saint, that's me
On my knees, giving you side eye—or am I?
The master of this altarpiece was so talented, his name
Lost to the ages—I saw to that. Why should "Anonymous"
Always be a woman? How do you like my ermine, the gold ring?

The head got slapped on a platter gaping like a dead fish.
Salome in yellow, very fetchingly, holds it like cold cuts.
She offers it to her kneeling guests.
Her mother asked for it, not I. The bodice on
Her gown hangs loose still, as if she just slipped it on after
A night of pole dancing at Herod's club.

I am just gazing at her as you gaze at the slimy buttocks of
A Kardashian on your phone screen. The head on the platter
Wears a halo. It's fabulous, fashion-forward.

Don't blame me for this atrocity. I just paid for the right
To stare with you at the wreckage from floor seats.
My hands are poised together, my lips slightly parted.
Christ have mercy, I seem to say, Lord have mercy.
Isn't this awful? It is, isn't it? Show me again.

JANUARY BUNKER

History so illuminates that
I don't need a flashlight down here, just this
Old-world glow. The Duc de Berry paid for
Art instead of war, a bright book of hours.
It gold-leafed the seasons. Peasant women
Gave sly looks as they curved down like their sheaves.
The Burgundy of the book, its bounties
Resplendent, masked knights turned to land pirates
After the king got kidnapped and would not
Return even when rescued. Other books
By clergy recommended ways to rape.
Plague ate enemies. The duke stayed home and read.
Behold, this book of hours on white vellum.
Outside, chaos agents abound, and yet—

FINDINGS AT THE REICHSTAG

After the fire, I poked through white ash,
Hoping some point would prove still solid.

Preserved in a charred tin box, I found a
Bakelite doll, feathers its hula skirt.
I blew. The down departed to reveal
Factory-tooled vulva, creased, painted brown.

I dug deeper and recovered foil-wrapped
Cigars. The tinsel declared: "It's a boy!"

After the fire, the hoses rolled again,
The balustrades and buttresses in dust,
We lumber out like the first reich, *alte Schule*—
The fleecers, the fist-fighters, the fuckers.
The Constitution in cinders, we turn
Feral, butterflying our foes' foreskins.

HAGGADAH FOLIO — THE TEN PLAGUES

I can't read Hebrew on this Alhambra
  Parchment, but the numbers are Arabic
Next to each illumination. How could
  This medieval Moorish master depict
Eleven-hundred years ago the plagues
  That we survive—*picta mirabilia?*

1) The plague of indifference

A man wreathed by a pink feather boa
Poses facing a mirror. Behind him,
A woman bearing a cup collapses.

2) The plague of frogs

This one appears straight out of Exodus
Until you see that the camel covered
In gold leaf is really a flat-bed truck.

3) *The plague of herpes*

I know! At first, those red spots look like gnats,
But the mountain where they hop and bite
Is no Sierra. Look at the peak!

4) *The plague of breakup*

The man crouches, his head between ruddy
Fists. He isn't crying. His expression
Remains impassive in his martyrdom.

5) *The Pestilence of livestock*

The woman is in front of that mirror,
Turned away, facing backwards, and frowning.
She grabs her buttocks, weighing melons.

6) *The plague of Boils*

This illumination, identical
To the third one, demonstrates one cannot
Escape one's past, not even with a balm.

7) The plague of AIDS

It's supposed to be a plague of thunder,
But this illumination streams sunlight
Through a window on a withered young man.

8) The plague of towers

A woman covered in dust crouches in a
Market square. She looks like a grey, hornless
Gargoyle. At her feet lies a black briefcase.

9) Darkness for Three Days

The illustrator ran out of pigments—
No vermillion, no *terre verte*—it looks like
An ashy Amazon, melted icebergs.

10) Death of Firstborn

The artist must have been smoking hashish.
He only drew the map of a vacant
Strip mall with a red dot marked *"You are here."*

DECEMBER BUNKER

One Christmas, I roasted chestnuts in the
Fireplace with my wonderful husband, Mark.
Only, I didn't have a fireplace. Mark
Divorced me. Chestnuts taste like wet cardboard.
But there I was roasting them, and my Mark
Was out caressing creases in crotches
While I shuffled the Nat King Cole carols
And watched the white flames making spirits bright.
Although It's been said many times, many
Times as an interrogation alibi,
In this tin hut, have yourself a merry
Little whatever you need next, darling.
Have yourself a merry contrarian.
This bunker is sound- proof. What do you need?

LOW ADOWN

"Who is it loves me? who loves not me?'/I would comb my hair till my
ringlets would fall/Low adown, low adown"
                                        —Alfred Lord Tennyson

A girl holds a book where mermaids wear crowns.
She learns the comb's direction—"low adown."
        Cruel schoolboys run in traffic. Principals
        scream outside—intersection low adown.
        They cheat. Pencils and blue books above desks,
        They palm-pass the correction low adown.
        How can I spray, my future a geyser,
        With my stream connection low adown?

Her lover rings. She buzzes him inside.
        She flings off shirts, discretion low adown.
        State polling places stuff ballot boxes.
        Candidates throw the election low adown.
        At the front gate, they strip him, tell him spread.
        Gloved hands perform inspection low adown.
        Married decades later, still stark naked,
        He feels his age, erection low adown.

Commercials lie about joint arthritis.
It feels like vivisection low adown.
　　　Near grandpa's bed the stepsisters whisper.
　　　"Cancer" they moan, inflection low adown.
　　　Tossing clods on coffins, we claim life lasts.
　　　The soul floats. Bones convection low adown.
　　　Libraries curate immortality.
　　　Authors pen retrospection low adown.

So I sit on my throne, mermaid alone,
　　　Still combing in reflection low adown.
　　　In this gesture, I brush a braille "Babson"
　　　On books, on tomb trajection low adown.

BRUNCH WITH LORD TENNYSON

Of course, I ordered him tea. I asked him if he preferred a mimosa or a bloody mary—I was guessing a bloody mary—and he told me

To some the drink becomes a light
That beckons from the cragged cliffs—
Not lighthouse but in storm's abyss
A siren tuning through the night.

So I ordered him some freshly-squeezed grapefruit juice instead, and I asked him if he preferred scrambled eggs with bacon or granola with fresh fruit, and he replied

When at last the morning broke afresh
And scattered gemstones in the dew
I woke. I walked and found things new
Though at dusk they seemed caught in mesh.
I marveled my nightmares had seemed true
When now the blazing cockatoo
Cawed loud in the souk at Marrakesh
And fez-capped men sought grains to thresh.

I asked the waiter if the couscous could be added to the brunch menu even though the lunch service started in a half hour, and he said yes. Overwhelmed by these surroundings, Fred said little. We held hands.

"Last night was surprising," I whispered, *"I hadn't expected, after the lecture…your beard tickled me."*

He leaned in and whispered back

Once again once again
Once again onward

The waiter brought our beverages, and he dropped my hand. He poured my tea.

PAJAMA PARTY WITH GERTRUDE STEIN

"But, Gertrude!" I implored, *"Why won't you let me gel your fingernails? Alice let me gel her toes, and you said she looked luscious!"*

Gertrude replied:
Luscious lunges much as luscious expunges.
A bower of lilies sillies and sullies a power.

She looked uncomfortable in the pink gingham nightshirt I had lent her. She kept her hair pulled back, wouldn't let me French braid it. Alice threw popcorn from the greasy bag at her during the movie—Gertrude's choice—*Un Chien Andalou*.

"Gertrude," I asked her afterwards, *"Now that we've seen Buñuel, Alice and I want to watch* Handmaid's Tale. *She says if you watch it, you can play the political asylum game with her when you get home. You like political asylum, right? Can't I stream it?"*

Gertrude sniffed:
A film is a film is a film, flim slim phlegm.

She did let me put a blue anti-aging mask on her, but she ate the cucumbers I put on her eyelids. Alice blue-toothed her playlist to my speakers, and she and I bopped to Billie Eilish while Gertrude gazed, unblinking.

I brought out some brownies from the kitchen, and Alice put her arms around Gertrude, and asked, *"So, honey, if you don't want to dance, what do you want to do?"*

I think very well of Billie but I do not know her name.
I think very well of Anne which is not the same.
How quickly they learn the quick learning.

She cut herself a slice of brownie and handed one to Alice, too. She sat on the edge of the bed. Her blue-masked jaw chewed quietly. Alice grinned like a monkey with brown goo on her teeth.

I laughed, but Gertrude did not. Alice and I looked at each other.

"Whatever," I sneered, rolling my eyes.

Whatever—Gertrude echoed.

ABOUT HANDS

I.

Melzer the manicurist counts clients in
A zoologist's field log. Hands flutter past
        Her face like errant butterflies loosed
        From their migration by the wafting of

Aromatherapeutic tonic decanted
In her water-smoothed, petal-pink fingerbowls.
        She catches them thus without a net,
        Beckons them, these pets of hers, by clicking

Her tongue, tisk-tisking at them. She lifts them to
The lamp at her station and eyes them from all
        Angles before she opens her box
        Packed with her dozens of delicate tools.

Call her their chronologist. She massages
Lotion reverently into the small of
        Each of them, each dollop a jewel
        Pressed and hidden in the palm, a fortune

Folded into the cookie. Yes, she charges
Market value for her services, but the
        Unrequited serenade painted
        Into each nail is a gift, a fruit of

The spirit. She squeezes one client between
Two others in the Manhattan walk-up where
        She practices, offering extras
        Gratuitously to faithful comers.

This is no immigrant struggle to Melzer
The manicurist, born in Honduras not
        Too long ago, transplanted to the
        South Bronx. To her, it is a sacrament.

II.

Hadassah is explaining her whole life to
The Israeli documentary team and
        Through the camera lens, to us all.
        What follows are only the subtitles:

"When we arrived at the Kibbutz, the ground was
Dry. I dug for weeds from light to sundown for
        Two decades. Look at these old hands now!"
        For the filmmakers' inspection, she spreads

Them out, the ancient parchments, the Dead Sea scrolls,
The Temple's Torah unrolled with the promised

      Prophesy to make the desert bloom.
      She reads them, and sighing, she continues:

"We had such trust in our beliefs! Who today
Would work like that now to end up with such claws?
      Not many. We weren't like salon
      Ladies, cutting our cuticles." The glow

Reemerges from her sharp eyes ringed by crows'
Feet, ancient, unfelled trees on her primeval
      Mountainside face. She smiles. "It was the
      Work we trusted to make us beautiful."

HEATHER LEWIS IN SEPTEMBER 1985

No. There was no sign of it as you strutted
In like a bull-dagger Elvis, tanned, buzz cut,
       Cigarette drooping out your mouth like
       A Bogart line from *The Maltese Falcon*.

No. You gave no hint of it as you turned the
Chair around, the butchest Marlene-Dietrich-
       Defiant attitude oozing out
       Your naughty smile, with double entendres

Worthy of the butchest, most diesel moment
Of Mae West's life, your oddly feminine hands
       Clenched in fists that looked tight and ready
       For any altercation the crowd sought,

No. You gave no clue to us that you were less
Than superwoman, a self-contained army
       From ancient Central Europe astride
       Wild horses, breasts missing for archer grips,

No. You didn't give us a chance, no guesses
That you were less than ironclad, that you cried

And howled, and sobbed, and snotted, and moaned
And needed us so much to pray for you

To patriarchal heaven and a male God,
The Creator of the universe Himself,
    The truest God and the butchest One,
    The One who taught you how to strut like that.

You would resent me for my commentary,
Yes. You might even beat the crap out of me,
    But Heather, you were just too cool to
    Go out like that, so can you blame me, grrl?

HOW AT AGE SEVEN I MET MARLENE DEITRICH'S CHARACTER

I.

She feels no love for children, especially
In color, not in black-and-white Weimar
      Cabaret shadow, where she sits misted.
      Her disdain, crooked lip, arched ironic
Brow plucked stiletto-thin over grease paint
And glare, to me it's *gemütlich*, a hug

Compared to my mother's bitter contempt
And her terror at my least plea. Ferocious
      As she is, a ghoul of *Deutches Kino*.
      Subtitled on Saturday afternoon
In shag-carpeted, paneled downstairs den,
My parents upstairs arguing again,

And she, a fishnet fiction *femme fatale*,
Fascist phantasm, well, she scares me less
      Than those upstairs, their final solutions
      Looming in long hallways without nightlights,
Not mass holocausts—much more personal—
Planning my oven end like Sylvia Plath,

Ach du, despairing of one another,
Wreaking any vengeance for any wrongs,
 And I, who (they say) while asleep, caused at
 Seven the *blitzkrieg* of my own home,
So I couldn't sleep, interrogated
With no right answers, only vague demands.

I could never offer alibis for
Waterboarding, drugging, dragging, me
 My mother's harangue that one day, I would
 Be a bad mother—so much worse than her,
A cult programming programme—bad mother
Bad mother, yes a bad muthah, mother.

I would be a bad muthah, not like her,
And if all school counselors and teachers
 Watched me faint from hunger, yet called no one,
 I must be a bad muthah already,
Birthing her bad self by herself, no midwife,
A bad mother, and not just at seven—

A badass motherfucker forever
World without end, amen, so hiding in
 Weimar republic, reading white letters
 Against grayscale, the sound of distant shouts
In their big house filled with mendacity,
Their loathing of me stinking like bacon,

What could Lola Lola do to me me?
As she sang growling, sobbing orgasm,
      What could Lola Lola do for me me?
        "What am I to do?" Lola Lola sang.
In pink pajamas, I fidgeted on the rug.
Lola Lola straddled a café chair.

I raised my hand high in the front row.
"Lola Lola?" I stretched forward, up.
      Lola Lola leaned back. *"Was ist es?"*
        "What am I to do?" I squeaked singing.
The music stopped, cabaret voided.
A holy virgin, a bad, bad muthah,

See I am assumed, not into heaven.
See I am assumed into churning reels,
      At the dark center of their mandalas,
        No midwife, no Mengele, no manners,
Scandalously savaging all space-time.
Bearing myself with a desperate push.

I arrive in a puff of cigarette—
A blue angel at *Der Blaue Engel.*
      So Lola Lola laughs laughs. *"Wilkommen!"*
        I don't speak German, but I speak Lola.
I speak bad mother. I speak cinema.
The lyrics I don't know yet, I can hum.

II.

In Weimar, they still keep the progressives.
I can smell the smoke of that cinema
Which burned around Dali's and Buñuel's
Un Chien Andalou, and in this dark room
With all the strangers and the flip-flipping,
I can walk to the moon and the slit eye,
But when will the beerhall *putsch* push me out?
I am featured in this film now for years.
Like most girl characters written by men,
I preen ageless, sexy, terrifying.
I entered this business at just seven,
But I wore the fishnets right away,
Straddled chairs knowing classified secrets.
I never cry here except when I croon.
I hope you won't mind my breaking the fourth wall,
But I want to know how it goes with you.
Did we ever beat the Nazis, really?
I can't see you clearly in the shadowed
Stadium seating, popcorn on your laps,
But are they gone for good? Are you sure?
It's just that I smell that smoke. Mae West
Keeps looking around so nervously,
And she knows that's a gun in your pocket!
If the allies won, why are you packing?
Marlene and I are sneaking out the

Jewish actors and wardrobe mistresses.
Emil Jannings, the male lead, he's brown-shirt.
We told him they died of the Spanish flu,
But he meets with a man with a notebook
Off-screen, and the expressionists have fled.
How is it out there? Safer where you are?
It doesn't look like it from here, my fans.
Remember—we strut around half-naked
Until that bitch Leni Riefenstahl and
Her crew make us cover up and salute!

III.

It's a wrap! In post-war post-production
Falling in Love Again—I never have kids.
Never wanted to—I fling my first fling
With a Russian Jewish boy fleeing

Muscovite knife fights—*What am I to do?*
Against his shower tiles—the first—I scream.
I buy a black kimono, and I strut
 Like Marlene Dietrich—*Can't help it.*

Love's always been my game—I match too much,
Too many, sadly, *play it how I may.*
But I am not afraid of fascists,
Even at my door. *I was made that way.*

I publish on racism—*can't help it.*
I give lectures about Weimar's lessons.
The Klan sends death threats for my trouble. *Men*
Cluster to me like moths around a flame.

I refuse to fear. I roll on fishnets.
And if their wings burn, I know I'm not to blame.

I'm middle-aged now, beyond the years of—
Falling in love again—straddling my chairs,

But I remain, just as it was foretold,
A bad muthah—*never wanted to.*
Tougher tougher than Lola Lola, more
Of a character—*can't help it.* The light

Hits my face, but I sit now in the dark.
I haven't really aged, but she has. Look!
You can see the cigarette burn that means
It's time to switch reels. That torch song scratches.

I haven't aged at all. I dance to hot jazz.
I string pearls, drink whiskey, don't be stingy.
Lola Lola is old old, older.
She wrecked the professor. The screenplay aged.

But read here. Here sprout my new words. I write
No creature of male imagination,

Not one of their sex monsters but my own,
Fiercer than what they could conjure. You read

Me, in a thick volume, full of secrets
Starlets only pretend to know—but know
Me here in black and white—the flesh made word,
Venus-of-Willendorf thick and holy.

Prefect bound, I straddle the a for "Anne"
And the z for the "zeitgeist," Weimar and why more
—a bad mother, a bad muthah mother—
Me! The smoke you smell is my book on fire.

COMMANDO LYRIC 3

After we planted nitro dynamite
Under the Claiborne Avenue bridge straddling
The industrial canal where they ship
The caged children to offshore factories,
Sydney, Jeannie, and I felt ecstatic.

We flopped onto each other, ecstatic
Under pirogue tarps. Some dynamite
Sticks shifted. We three felt like factories
Of explosive heat, blowing up friendship
Into smoky panting exhaled straddling

Border crossings, straying off-trail straddling
Work and play, war and love—so ecstatic!
We three passed so close to death—Chiron's ship
Reserved state rooms for us on dynamite-
Planting nights. They had no prints, these factories,

Only our blurred shadows on factory
Webcams, but the cops still smelled us straddling
Our graves. The thrill of it sparked dynamite!
Back in town, Sydney and I, still ecstatic,
Started kissing near the New Orleans ship

Drydock. We kissed Jeannie, who worshipped
Us both. We streaked into that factory
Abandoned on Tchoupitoulas, ecstatic
From the taste of each other's skin, straddling
And cupping one another's dynamite.

Later, when Sydney left, on Canal Street,
Jeannie leaned into me, sighed, "smell my hands!"
I lifted them each up to my nostrils:
Citrus nitroglycerine and oil soot
Infused sweat-juice shed releasing captives.

FEBRUARY BUNKER

Nothing grows in this season but yearning,
But instead of frost or brown patches,
I painted a diptych of daffodils.

On one panel, I sit as I do here now,
Only in a field where a hart eats them.

On the other, I kneel before David,
Patron saint of Wales, who holds a pigeon.

I shoo away birds with yellow bouquets.

I'm a protestant. I don't revere him.

Someone pounded on the door this morning.
Then, I heard a distant scream.

Yellow flowers can so cheer up a room.

THE SAINT

A face in the stained glass now, you glance down
placidly from an arrow-slit window, with black lines
for eyes glazed over an illuminated butternut nugget,

at me. Martyr, what does suffering look like from there?
When Harold Lloyd and Charlie Chaplin flicker on screen,
skid down slick surfaces, no recording of their screams,

mortals in three dimensions and surround sound laugh.
So expanded now, in new dimensions and color, do you
see our near disasters as comedy? Have you forgotten

the blood blisters, the whole town glowering at you,
failure where failure is not a sacrifice, but only shame?
Have you forgotten the arrows burning your own flesh?

Things look cleaner from a distance. From the bleachers, the fans
cannot see the field's ruts, and if the players were unnumbered,
if they did not sport uniforms, and if no vendor hawked programs

in the stands, the men sliding around the diamond, stretching
for the pop fly, pounding their fists into their gloves, would look
    leisurely.
Sweat isn't visible from the sky box. The organ plays a fight song,

or is it a hymn? From where you hover, above me kneeling a run
into my stocking, wheezing in the dust from the unswept pew,
perspiring in my polyester best, I must look as serene as you do.

AT THE SCUOLA DI SAN ROCCO

The gate guard greeted me "*pronto*," not "*buongiorno*,"
As if I were afar off phoning, but there I
Stood, *ecce homo*. Years, this artist contributed

As dues a painting. He lived long. There are no blue
Periods. The vanishing point remains in
Place, never flattened by fattening fingers. The

Light and shadow dance to the same tune, as if all
Painted the same summer, with the same music on
The same club jams radio station blaring, but

The tune was caught in his head, not in the waves of
The Grand Canal — these the exorcisms thereof.
Today, critics would whine "Demoded; stuck in a

Rut." Then, though, the rich lava moved with the cooling
Volcano weight of the dark velvet curtains dragged
Along marble. Then, here, the fastest path between

Two local points was a gondola punt through curved
Canals that intertwine like fingers folded in
Penitent prayer. Birth was cruel, ripping, literal,

No *vaporetto* trip down a curved, quaint canal,
Eve's curse to these women in the heavy dresses.
Death, however, was only a metaphor for

A side-winding trip to purgatory or, for
One uninvolved in *doge* intrigues, a faster arc
Upward toward that light piercing the rain cloud. The school

Is shut but for these canvasses. Today, Turks like
Me shoot with cell phone cameras, post to Facebook,
Use a navigation tool that leads us away.

MY AFTERNOON WITH LAURA INGALLS

My mother's suitcase rests feet from the front door
She threatens to leave because we "leech her freedom."
      Not fed by family, I faint blood-hungry.
      I collapse in family restaurants — no food.

On tiptoe, I grab books, sneak out to the hammock.
I shake it loose of leaves and spiders to slip in
      Between two pine trees, suspended slightly above
      The underbrush and its rustling, the troubled muck.

I hear more shouting in the house. Nobody looks
For me right now, so the blood blame ricochets blank,
      And out here, I can drive a team of dark horses
      To that other house, the cabin on the Prairie,

Too small to closet my modern problems, but still
Troubled — snow to the second floor, drifting for weeks,
      Scarlet fever, malaria, drought, locusts. Those
      Problems have names. A girl could starve respectably

In blizzards, not like here, on a Spring cul-de-sac.
In this big backyard, I get called the problem names.

The problem remains incognito. My mother screams,
Screams again, muffled. I open chapter fourteen.

She pops out at me, calico-wrapped, bonneted.
"Have you ever read *Huckleberry Finn*?" I ask.
    She shakes her head no. "Let's build a raft!" I demand.
    We bundle sticks, firewood, pool cues, jump ropes,

Some plywood in the back of the garage, duct tape.
She sits on the pile while I wrap rope around it all.
    I empty Elmer's glue. We stand back, examine.
    Watching it dry, I ask Laura, "Where's the river?"

The bonnet covers her face. She stares at her boots.
There is a well where a bad girl could drown herself.
    But on the prairie, there is no Mississippi.
    The glue grows less tacky. She and I climb aboard.

Nothing moves two little girls stuck in the driveway.
Little girls running away run into traffic.
    The water does not flow for us, floating us North.
    We sit there in the driveway, dirty and inert.

My mother's suitcase stays anchored in the hallway.
Glue fastens my pants. My fingers clam together.
    Run aground, no rescue in sight, I slouch back in.
    An anemic leech, starving in muck, I get stuck.

I sneak upstairs to my room, search chapter fifteen.
My mother slams the front door over and over.

MAY BUNKER

Before I came down here, days before—you know—
I rode the Saint Charles streetcar from one end
Of the line to the other. I watched girls
In uniforms descend near Loyola.

Old ladies struggled near Napoleon
To catch a rail ride to the pharmacy.

At the terminus, the few who remained
Got off forgotten. Then after—you know—
As I ran for the first basement, then walked
Down to the second, then so low beneath
It, all hesitation-stepped to the last door,
The end of the line, knowing this was it.

I thought about how the driver just strolls
From one end of the vehicle to the
Other and reverses its path, but first,
Before driving back to the other end,
They make you wait. It feels like forever.

BEFORE

I spoke their language as a philosopher.
      I assumed harsh consonants accidents.
I stood in long lines at their communions.
      They laid hands on. I listened, bent forward.
I sat under their lectures, taking notes.
      They seemed clean, free of the stain of questions.
They dressed so nicely, invited me out—
      Beerhall nights where we polkaed like partners.

Oh, forgive me! I took them at their word.
      "Call me but love," I exclaimed up toward
The dark balcony, thought myself baptized,
      Once more, But the baptismal font was dry.
I waited in white, their favorite color,
      But their full immersion required drowning.

A CONFEDERACY OF OBJECTS:

The bronze statue, a soldier's folded arms;
    The pewter trinket, monogrammed F-U;
    The paper pom-pom, crinkling red and blue;
    The lady's bracelet, jingling tangled charms;
    The foam hand, finger pointed heavenward;
    The shotgun, dusted, rusted on a rack;
    The tea tray, laden with a larded snack;
The button: "Vote for Boudreaux, Seventh Ward;"
    The battered jam jar, lethal shine inside;
    The stovetop griddle, still stuck with batter;
    The frayed leggings, strained as thighs got fatter;
    The decayed trailer, rotting double-wide.;
    The flag: the starred bars crossed like barbed gateposts;
Rusted sign: whites only — Stand back, lynched ghosts.

WOMAN SHOT ON FONTAINEBLEAU DRIVE

"A woman was shot Tuesday night... Police were looking at the intersection of Fontainebleau and Versailles Boulevard, where a small kitchen knife, a pack of cigarettes and scissors were lying next to the sidewalk."

—The Times Picayune, May 11, 2016

Next to the chalk outline: a paring knife;
Next to the casement: fourteen lucky strikes;

Curbside, where the blood spattered: sewing shears;
In the gutter: a crushed pepperoni;

In the grass crack in the asphalt: a brooch;
From the window above: double dutch ropes;

Hanging from power lines: scuffed Air Jordans;
Across the street, where one witness screamed: grits;

Under a truck parked nearby: torn gingham;
Three doors down: an old tabasco bottle;

In the storefront church: moldy carpet tiles;
At the Shell station: Cartons of moon pies;

On Fontainebleau Drive: the woman shot; the Uniforms; the gloves; the bags; the questions.

LOSING MY VIRGINITY AFTER THE EIGHTH GRADE FORMAL

I.

After that cafeteria dance, I
Pursed my oversized fish-mouth—not through a
Funhouse mirror—through a funhouse self, leaned
      Toward my mirror to poke my nose for zits.
      What hid behind this thin chin, that anxious
      Glare? Could it hide a moustache's shadow,
      Blank though my punk-rock-party-girl skin gleamed?
      An old, cracked mirror back, rust-corroded,
      Double-reflected his slow, sallow smirk,
His hat tipped in ironic chivalry.
"And they keep asking you whether you're a
Melanie or Scarlett, don't they?" he quipped,
"You know better, though, don't you, Bonnie Blue?"
I did. I remembered—somehow—when I
Wall-flowered in a corner by myself,
He waltzed with me, pressed against, pressed through me.
How we danced divinely—oh, one body!
Those overheated lips, my lips, grazed neck.
Muscled fists grabbed thighs, my tawny nipples,
          His, nibbled, nuzzled, double-entrendred
My rosebud sex to strum the honeybee—

Enjambments, enjambments, oh, the envoi!
We snarled we were not the marrying kind.
He cupped my burgeoning curves afterwards,
While I flipped through his chest hairs, word-searching.

As Leda to swan, Bull to Europa,
I, Zeus, I nymph—I Mason, I Dixon,
As Captain Rhett Butler, I fucked myself.
A Yankee ambush and a John Wilkes Booth,
I united my states and popped my cherry.
Like Washington, I cannot tell a lie.
Double-sexed as an earthworm, I shed grace
On my own purple mountains, amber waves.
I was South risen again in Brooklyn,
Pirate and scalawag, parry and thrust,
Bodily fluid, bodily fluid,
Both girl child and fancy man in twin bed.

II.
We still cross each other at social functions.
        Other guests look slightly uncomfortable.
We both possess suspicious Yankee ties.
        He runs blockades, and I break glass ceilings.
Dressed like cads, we preen, lean against mantles,
        Staring too hard as others pass our way.
Embracing lost causes and wayward ones,
        We tell outrageous truths. We joke to hide.

Both of us remain merely the figment
      Of a sad woman's imagination.
We reconstruct no real place in the South.
          Haven't you heard, my dear? We aren't received!

NATIONAL FRONT DREAM JOURNAL

July 14—Nothing. July 15—I dreamt
A field of brown goats. I took out my Swiss knife and
Gutted them all. They wanted to run, I
Could see in their eyes, but they stood obedient.

July 16 I lay in bed between sleep and
Waking and remembered my mother, her
Caress with a black bar of soap on my white skin.
July 17—Nothing. July 18—No—

Thing—well—nothing. July 19—I was in a
Sugar cane field, whip in hand, but there was no one
To whip but myself and the stalks above my head.
I awoke weeping. July 20—You asked

Why I kept this journal. My white princess, it's so
You understand one day. July 21—Nothing.
July 22—Nothing. July 23—
I dreamt of Joan of Arc, clad in armor, standing

Above me in her stirrups. I called her my lady.
She spat in my face again. I woke up laughing.

July 24—The children's screams when I ripped
Them out of their mothers' arms were my lullaby

Tonight. I cradled my pillow and hummed our song.
July 25—You call this genocide, but
These aren't *gens*. Call it germicide, and I will
Buy your brother a beer. Call it a love letter!

Last night, I dreamt of you. I was fucking you. We
Started out making love, but you laughed, demanded
I fuck harder and harder until I was all
Covered in your clear-water sweat and even

Your blood, which smelled like dandelions. You stopped laughing.
July 26—Why won't you return my calls
Or even text me back? Don't you know I do all this
To preserve you inviolate? July 27—

August fifteenth is the Feast of the Virgin once
Again. Will you be there? Look for me, my princess,
In procession carrying the box of secret
Relics behind men who bear the statue. I will

Find you. I dreamt last night again of your blood all
Over me, but found only the dandelions.
July 28—Don't you realize that the
Others lack imagination? That is why they

Give me special tasks. When they see me in the hall,
They slap me on the right shoulder and call me "bro,"
but they have stopped making eye contact. Not since—you
Know I can't tell you. Last night, I dreamt of it. Waking,

I remembered how bad raw liver smells before
You add caramelized onions to the pan. I
dreamt of cooking, you know, it—all of it. I fed
It to my terriers, then felt jealous of them.

July 29 —Nothing. July 30—
Nothing—the ineffable—it's bigger than us.
July 31—You finally called back! You
Have always been mine. I am thinking right now of

Your skin, how light shines through it from the bones inside,
Luminously white, how your albino blondeur
Crowns you like daisies. That one nuzzle I stole from
You at the last rally? What I liked best about

Your blonde—it smelled like nothing. Your whole white being
Is an empty page on which I can write verses.
You must know how I love you! I dedicate all the
Crushed knuckles to you. All the special projects I

Can't mention? They are yours in tribute, enemy
Foreskins! I emailed your father again, asking

Him to grant you to me. I offer him some heads,
that he can name their nappy nationalities.

He must be mulling that over. He understands.
Last night, I dreamt of your nothing, the nothing I
Make of you, the defense of your nothing against
All the ink in the world but mine, invisible ink

That appears when a flame nears the paper, waking
the yellow message, and on you, I had written
The special projects, all of them, the tools I used,
The sounds they made, the messes I cleaned afterwards,

And you became my box of secret relics, the
Body parts of the virgin uncorrupted, so
Immaculately white, above all white, and I
Took charge of them, walked through the streets with the treasure

Of them, and you, my white princess, were my shining
Armor, scabbard to my white metal gutting knife,
And, oh! How I loved you even more than I loved
The special projects, even more than I love the

Empty fragrance of your hair, even more than the
Reenactment of each dream in my journal here,
My white virgin, my white page, my white canvas
For the visceral grease paint of my masterwork!

SEPTEMBER BUNKER

I flip the folio to the *Man of Sorrows*
Of the Duke and Duchess of Savoy. They
Mutely observe Christ excruciated,
Wounded, standing on a lower green alp,
A blue chateau behind him, a lake, and
Behold! Jesus bleeds in all this beauty.
The Latin inscription — this can't be right!
I think it says: *"I have lost track of crimes*
This year, and I will give praise. My God is
Small but is aided by my story." No,
I never studied Latin formally.

I must have it backwards. Who would write that?
Before I combination-locked myself
In here, America packed babies in
Boxes, wrapped them in foil, and they all wailed.
The Dukes of Hazzard and Amarillo
Flanked them left and right, stared down passively
And blamed the other party for their pain.
Lord, I, too, have lost track of crimes this year.
I am buried like Faust in my books. But
I sell no souls. My God is not small. He
Figures prominently in this, my story.

WHY

We shake our fists at your mottled gray sky
Demanding what others have demanded:
A reasonable explanation why
When bullies flout what you have commanded,
Why you don't descend, rattle rifles, cry,
"Defy me? You shall be reprimanded!"
Why, instead, you shine the summer sun, sigh
Lazy breezes over corpses landed
Newly on the killing pile—stacking high
Human incense held out underhanded,
Incense offered to you to putrefy
Beneath your nostrils yet unoffended
By the stench of new massacres, the fly
Feast of blood, the stink of the latest lie.

COMMANDO LYRIC 2

Mad walked with me wheat pasting one evening.
  "Put on your shiny dress. Wear rhinestones,"
I instructed. That way, they'd presume us
   Just hookers headed to those brass soirees

On Clara Street near the Superdome.
   Mad whipped out one of our posters for peace.
I held up tail ends of my fox stole like wings,
   Shading her movements. I giggled loudly,

"Oh! Quit it!" then whispered, smiling barred teeth,
   "Cops!" Mad peered over my faux fur fence. *"Cops?"*
Where?" I tilted my head right, swinging my
   Earring. *"Two o'clock. Two men in denim."*

"Cops? No! Construction workmen, don't you think?"
   "After six pm? Cops!" One lifted his
Coffee to his lips. Mad saw his holster.
   "Cops," I hissed again, straightening her hems
As if we shared swanky destinations,
   Chock-full of champagne and vodka cocktails.

Down here, I have stocked plenty of champagne.

I will save it for the last evening.

Either I drink it with liberators,

Or I make Molotovs out of bottles.

GRAVEYARD SHIFT

Behind the office tower greens a graveyard
where the city has long stopped grieving
the Spanish Jewish dead of days before faxes,
centuries before software, time before Timex.
As the copy machine collates, the granite letters
curl like palm fronds into Aleph, Chai, Gimmel, Beth,
and the relief receptionist threads a headset through her
hair weave as the moldering bones creep into the roots of
magnolia trees — Magnolias in Manhattan! — and ride up
xylem and phloem into swooning petals. The memo circulates
     while
seraphim shaped like homeless Gulf War vets speak in   tongues,
tell the temps on lunch break: Some day, you'll rot in a yard like
     this
no relatives remembering, and those dictations you take, they'll
     weigh less
than the dust of your toenails, and won't you be happier here?

MARCH BUNKER

A hound at my feet,
I type these lyrics.
He eats the roaches.
I keep him for this.

       Out there—the thunder.
       The dog barks. He leans
       On my legs. I type.
       He hates the crashing.

       In here, I draft.
       I wonder just who
       Will ever hear
       what I write while

       The thick layers of
       Insulation
       Seal us both in.
       I draft, redraft.

DRY MARTINIS AT THE NATIONAL ARTS CLUB

Sitting pretty on this heavy-leather high-backed
Throne, a thick Persian carpet pillowing each step
Of my alligator stilettos, the oak of
The paneling blackened by the weight of passing
Years where nothing of note changed here, not for the worse,

Cupping the clean cone of the clean glass, its vermouth
Refractions interrupted just delicately
By the magnified trio of olives on the
Rosy toothpick, I could forget all my rough drafts
And imagine that each of my verses had been
Born in perfect cadence as I exhaled gently

Yesterday, that each opus of my life required
No more perspiration than it takes to hail a
Cab on Grammercy Park South after a brilliant
Function. You know I am a member of the club.
Turtlenecks and ascots are not acceptable
Substitutes for neckties for the gentleman, and
My legs may be exposed by the length of my skirt
But not sausage-skinned in leggings or stirrup pants.

I pay my dues, and although no hard currency
Changes kid-gloved hands within these portrait-patched walls,
The pantheon expects a monthly check from me.

Don't believe what they say—you never stop feigning
A casual disdain as you look over your
Shoulder to see if the doorman has finally
Caught on to you. Each poem is held up at the

Latest auction, and the old ladies guarding the
Till whip out their lorgnettes, the jewelers their loupes,
And the bidding always starts at the minimum.

MY FACE AS A DAMAGED MANUSCRIPT

The skin—rubbery and bouncing back rocks.
The nose—grime-greased and swine-like.
The skin—again, yes—wilted, long unkissed.
The gaze—gray from the bottom of a lake.
This reflection, caught in terra cotta
Pans catching river runoff from unseen

Leaks, shows me now crumbled, once a pearl,
Now petroglyph in this cement Lascaux.
Will I ever be dug up, examined?
A French woman giving me a facial
A decade ago told me Earth preserves.
I would be dead by now above ground, yes.

But isolated here, sediments form.
Time makes my face hold *pietra dura*
Evidence of layers of trauma carving
Me into an odd illumination.
It's not just some fine lines. It's the worry
I have hidden from everyone but me.

I am its witness. This bunker may be
My shelter, but I have hidden decay

Buried from the chaos, sequestered like
Silverware stashed from Yankee soldiers,
Only I am the one thrown down the well.
The assets sit ripe for plucking above.

My face is hidden. I can remember
A jazz club mirror. Through a glass darkly.
I saw red lips, eyeliner sweated off.
The mouth flashed a confident woman's smile.
She seduced whom she pleased, whispered curses
In hot ears, stuck her tongue in some of them.

This face is a remnant with lacunae,
The Anglo-Saxon poem "The Ruin,"
In flesh, at least its watery shadow,
A submerged ancient Grendel that yet lurks
Where *Beowulf* shouted "*Hwaet*" and fought it,
My face undefeated, hoarded treasure.

HOW THINGS HAVE GOTTEN TO THIS POINT

While tyrants stalk us, ardent academicians
Bury their noses deeper in their dusty books
And ignore our shouts in the street for physicians
For this sick city. "*Yes,*" these inveterate schnooks
Mutter to themselves in the library's corners,
"*I'll write an article about this injustice*
For a geopolitical journal!" Mourners
Wail outside the window of the flying-buttressed
Ivory tower, but these thinkers' protest march
Is to the stacks, not to the bunkers, not to fight,
Not even with their words, in the bloodied boulevards.
Today's *Christalnacht* is tomorrow's chapter's note,
Not a wrong to right today—just a new wrong wrote.

NOVEMBER BUNKER

It would be damp and frigid outside now.
Pressurized chambers here don't lose their leaves.
Bindings tighten, preserved beyond my time.
I squat slumped on dark concrete tiles between

My wine cave and the shelves Sloane and Cotton.
Parchments got blotched with marginalia,
Scribal interventions, killer rabbits,
Jailed virgins walking dragons on leashes—

Saint Margaret figures prominently—
But not me. I decant a burgundy
And a Burgundian law book. I squint.
It must be freezing outside—I recall,

Sip communion as if it were not blood.
I try to shiver—the way my fingers

Once numbed on the windshield as I scraped it
With my expired credit card, no gloves on,

As the slush soaked through the feet of my tights.
If my memory could freeze up down here

Into a cone dripping from the rafters,
This underground would frame a cozy life.

ACTUAL NIGHTMARES I HAD AS A TODDLER

"Why are you crying, Anne?" a syrupy voice asks.
A stranger's hands near to change my diapers.
She grabs the waistband and pulls it. I flail.

On my family patio, slurping
Melted Ice cream, I slump, suddenly blind.
"She's not breathing!" I hear my cousin shout.
I know I am dead. This doesn't bother me.

With an animated beige body like
Wendy's from *Peter Pan*, I have little
Apple breasts ripening through my nightgown.
They heave. I cannot move. Captain Hook has
Lashed me to the mast. A thick bullwhip cracks.

I scream and leap out of bed. Parents rush in.
I explain, *"I can't get a PhD until I
Am at least twenty-eight. What if all the
Egyptian mysteries get solved by then?"*

I sit in a white parked car. Momma shops.
A shadowy man in a trench coat and
Cowboy hat stares at me through the windshield.
I stare back. I smile. He smiles back. I ask,

"Are you here to kill me?"

"Not yet," he whispers.

I WAKE FROM A DREAM IN THE BUNKER

In the dream, I stand outside with Lisa.
We are laughing like nothing's gone wrong.
She is wearing a chartreuse fedora.

Waking here, I'm a toreadora,
Waving pages like capes all day long.
In the dream, I stand outside with Lisa.

Down here, with Plutarch, *sono sola*.
Verse echoes off concrete, a gong,
Lo stil nuovo indossa un fedora.

Hunched over down here, leaning Pisa,
My towering writers all throng.
In the dream, I stand outside with Lisa.

In that dream, I sprout fresh as freesia,
New thoughts from medieval mud spawned,
I am wearing a chartreuse fedora.

It's spring, provided one has amnesia,
Recalls no Beerhall Putsch ping pong.
In the dream, I stand outside with Lisa.
She is wearing a chartreuse fedora.

MUSICAL NEWSREELS

I think I am the brunette with
Big earrings tearily singing
La Marseillaise in the face of the
Nazis at Rick's (everybody
Goes there). But what if I am shocked,
Shocked to discover gambling in

My precarious hour in this
Smoky room? Do I smile instead,
A prim Nazi conductor of
An Oompa-pa brass orchestra
Who taps his baton on the stand
And grins into their government

Camera, promoting pop art
Allowed by oppressors, airy
As the music plods — no more swing
Allowed, and we can't dance because
It's not our revolution—or
Am I revolutionary?

Do I accompany the band
Of Gestapo thugs who grab babes

From arms because I write music
Or sing it, wave a baton, not
A machete to lop off heads?
Aux armes, Citoyens! Or am I
Just the end-of-the-world lounge act?

One-two-three:
This polka,
This is dance,
Isn't it?
People clap,
So I think,
        Because they
        Like music,
        But are they
Signaling
Gun muzzles
In their backs?
        An artist
        Such as I
        Think I am
Makes them smile,
Or do I?
Is that fear?
        A grimace?
        We don't swing.
        No improv!

Oom-pa-pa
Prosody,
Serving the
> Fatherland,
> After all,
> Don't we just
Love the beat
Even when
Beat is down,
> Downbeat down,
> The beatdown?
> They beat down
Enemies
Of the State
While I stretch
> Baton out
> And I wave
> It midair.
Trumpets play
While I smile—
While I smile.

POEM WHERE I AM A RELIQUARY, A *VIERGE OUVRANTE*

Full disclosure: I haven't been a sacred vessel for a long time.
I am empty, as you can see through the glass.
They have lit me just so. Hushed patrons shuffle by.
Some point. Others gesture toward larger urns.

I am supposed to contain the fetus Jesus, to be His
Tabernacle. I am supposed to be a virgin.
I was handled by too many silversmiths in my making
For me to remain one, really. They wiped off prints

When they poised me next to the index card labeling me.
I am empty. I said that before, but it bears repeating.
I am an evacuated Heavenly Jerusalem.
I am descending to Earth in the End Times.

I am a trope, a symbol *ex-machina*.
I am mineral. I utter *Magnificat*.
But a woman? Don't believe it!
Butter wouldn't melt in my mouth.

OCTOBER BUNKER

I am writing all this down, every last bit of it.

I Type? I pound! Is the keyboard on fire? I may pop the letters off!

The dog is barking into a dark corner—at what?

Here I yowl into the night calling for a pack I have lost running
away.

Who is my audience? Who on Earth dares to sign for this parcel?

Who would John Hancock this declaration in a time like this?

ERRANDS

I went to
Key Food last night in search of Hemingway—
You know, the way Ginsberg found
Whitman in the produce aisle pinching the long zucchini—but
Papa was nowhere, not even gnawing on a roast turkey leg in
       the deli section.

Later, I found him sitting on the back stool of the basement
       bar nearby.
We split a bourbon.
His hand shot to my thigh in less time than it took for me to
       down the first sip.
He described the entire fight against
Franco, all the boiling blood and screaming stallions, in short
       sentences.
He declared all his lion hunts — the smell of curare and
Sweaty men in pup tents, the primeval triumphs—
In a staccato of one-syllable words.
I asked, "But what about the adjectives?
Were they rationed in the war?"
He explained what he learned from boxing
Gertrude Stein—that a gun is a gun is a gun.
He staggered up, made it into the john, and killed himself again.

Today, Virginia Woolf and I ran into each other at
Rite Aid Drugs in the feminine protection section.
We talked about him in run-on sentences, using "heliotrope" and
"Saharan" in flying buttress phrases.
We said it figured, with that
Guernica grammar, that he was suicidal, promised to brunch—me
        and you, her and
Vita—and we both made it home alive.

TO SYLVIA PLATH

Sylvia, you tortured laurel, Daphne frozen
By her father on the Northeast Industrial
Mud bank to stop the long-awaited free exchange
Of Godly bodily fluids, Siren atop
The cliff of the MacMillan Publishing Building
Drawing the mariners along the Hudson from

Sarah Lawrence poetry workshops to you still,
I put wax in my ears, you lousy Lorelei,
You're no *Colossus* astride my city any
Longer. You're no *Ariel*, inspiring some old
Prospero to incant. No! You've robbed me, skank, of
Every other member of my sophomore class.

Every time a writer's block hits, someone whips
Out razor blades to scribble the bloom you wrote in
The bath water. Sylvia, you made me wear black
Patent leather heels to high school, cross gravel and
Tracks in stiletto heels, despite the rose blisters.
And now I wear black everywhere. I've outstrolled

The path you set for me to some London suburb's
Oven by half a decade, but I'm still going

To funerals for the brilliant women you've lured
To your flytrap lair of Lorelei lyric lies.
The directors of mortuaries wink at me
As if to say, "next!" in the Second Avenue

Deli takeout line. Here's my order: One pound of
Kosher forbearance. Spiced tongue, no need to slice it,
One of those sandwiches, the kind your mouth never
Quite wraps around, stuffed with all the things the next years
Will bring me instead of your prescribed demise, hold
The sour pickle. Sylvia, wraith, death-breath-bimbo,

I'm living to collect my Pulitzer to spite
You, you friggin' chicken-livered lily-pusher!
I'm going to live to see the bottoms of my arms
Wobble when I stretch them out to embrace my great-
Grandchildren. The love handles won't stop me dancing
At my later birthdays, even though you've thinned out

The guest list considerably. Sylvia, you
Are my Third World War, stealing my generation's
Most brilliant and a host of others too scared to
Fire back at you from the trenches, a high stack of
Casualties in cocktail dresses piled beside
My bed every night to pray for, whose rigor

Mortis hands have dropped their pens and now just reach for
My ankles when I get up in the middle of
The night for the bathroom. I gasp, then tell them to
Drop me. Now I don't belong to them, to you, to
Sexton, to the other women writers who have
Impaled themselves on the pens they brandished for far

Too short a time. I remind them who I am, not
Who tonight, but whom I must presume to be: last
Testifier to all that killed the others and
Locked the jaws of the ones who quit their words. They let
Go. I pee, then sleep to write tomorrow's poem.

THE NIGHT BAUDELAIRE RAN HIS FINGERS THROUGH MY HEAD OF HAIR

It lay on a pillow frizzing. The room splayed humid.
    Hurricane. Hurricane. Hurricane. Hurricane.
    My skin warmed. I woke jolting. Something

Brushed me. Dozing, I remembered verses
    About his flamboyant, honest continent—
    Women and men preened wildly in

Sultry tropics rimmed by ardent geysers
    The global warming, the warming global,
    Telling each other hot-mouthed truth at last,

All through the wormhole of his lover's kinky curls.
    He wanted to wave her hair, an unfurled flag
    Of his new, naked nation, but here, in America,

O'er the ramparts we watched, all we could see,
    Oh so gallantly streaming, were my slightly
    Wiry waves of grain- yellowed sprouts from

A slightly sweaty scalp, a wave but no warp
    Or woof, no whitherly—just Becky's good hair,

No baseball bat smashed into the windshield,

No overflowing floodwaters wetting orange hems,
        Just split ends the color of corn husks, just muted
        Deep-conditioned, triple-processed, highlighted
        white-girl...

He yanked his fingers away after an aborted comb-through.
        The balding poet was so disappointed—No
        Eve wreath of flowering vines to wilt, nor evil
        blossoms

Burning like dry ice—just fashion victim
        Over-sprayed eighties over-sprayed Madonna
        Frizz disappointed, even in 1984,

Was that Orwell shaking his head, too?
        Madonna wannabe, Rhonda, help help me,
        More Cinnabon cruller than volcanic cruelty,

More blonde Madonna than whore of Babylon,
        And the great poet demoniac in a pique
        Sniffed like a cat sprayed with water
        And evaporated in a poppy smoke

JULY BUNKER

The fan oscillates, rustling my pages.

They whisper Whitman's ferry-crossed seagulls.

They take me back to Brooklyn, years ago,
When I stood in the dark on Seagate beach,
My dress blown against my hot skin. I breathed.

The ocean breathed. The man held his thin breath.

A neighbor, he hoped against hope, I would
Love him as myself. But instead, I let
A cable clang against a chain link fence.

NO TRESPASSERS, the sign spelled in all caps
Under the streetlamp. I listened to waves
Drowning out his line. The wind undid words.

Down here, the ink remains indelible.
Every syllable counts. No nature
Interrupts their imperatives down here.

NO TRESPASSERS—no trespassers trespass.

FROM THE CONVENT AT HEFLA

Ghandi said, *"Be the change you wish to see."*

Here, we feed the orphans, go nurse the sick.

For you, that means, "Pretreat your own laundry."

It means, "Wash those plates in the sink yourself."
Call me a feminist, call me mystic—
I don't care. You're afraid of all women
Who won't sleep with you, nuns or just fed up.

Little black dress or black habit—the same
To you either way—the bitches cock block.

We also cook block. We won't fry your fat.

We're kneeling here doing nothing that serves
You, not that you can see. You watch pots boil
Over and wait for the women to wipe.

Keep waiting. We won't run back with a rag.

WHERE LOUIS, LESTAT AND I BAR-CRAWL BOURBON STREET

Whatever words say, bodies govern us,
Trapped by flesh, no matter which pretty speech.
But on Bourbon, bouncers don't card this
Child corpse. They assume I'm auditioning.
I watch women spin on poles, cellulite
Jiggling while they twerk, fat nipples bouncing.
Louis and Lestat slip into the lounge,
But I am not hungry for the buffet.
I stole a wallet off my midnight snack
On Conti. I slip bills in g-strings, not
To satisfy appetites, but to watch
Women's thighs show me stretch marks and track marks
Through bronze spray tan, tattoos, and glitter sweat.

This book freezes me in glitter amber.
My child vampire body will never grow.
That's not vampire blood. That's vampire novel.
I ask Britni, the one I panty-stuffed
With twenty singles, to answer questions.
What's her favorite book? She doesn't read.
Not reading books traps, too, I see. Britni

Won't reach fifty, my night vision tells me.
But what is your favorite book? Yes, you there!
And to what has it taught you to submit?

MONTHLESS BUNKER

I have camped out down here a minute. The
Wine from Galatoire's is half-drunk by now.
The dog grew some new grey whiskers, sleeps more.
My firm handshake has gone now noodle-limp.
I recall kissing, but not with whom.
That said, I am surrounded by beauty.

I pasted gilded illuminations
On black slabs, as screen savers, months ago.
I am prefect bound with them now, giving
Sly side eye like that Luas Cranach Eve—
Over there scotch-taped to the china hutch—
Staring at the snake, who tells her Eden

Has her walled up and *"Ye shall not surely*
Die: For God doth know that in the day ye
Eat thereof, then your eyes shall be opened"
I have camped out down here a minute. It's
Tempting to know good from evil outside.
What would a peek above cost me, really?

But I am not innocent, like Eve was.
I know all about the walls. They hold back

North America's longest river, and
I don't only mean the Mississippi.
Jim looked up it and saw freedom, but he
Did not jump off of the raft and swim toward it.

I have a first edition signed by Twain.
See? The library banned it long ago.
I sneaked it out during Spring Break back then.
There are dogs, not just my dog, and bullets.
I stay on the raft. My dog eats the snake.
My eyes face forward once more toward pages.

THE EVENING STOLEN FROM THE GREAT POET

Of course, students, I knew him at first glance.

In surprise, his forehead wrinkled into a fourteen-line
        Petrarchan sonnet,
Ronsardian in its yearning,
The second he apprehended my approach:
Jiggling,   twenty-three,   braless, nipples upturned
Like two periscopes winking suggestively,
Two trembling mongooses waiting for the big snake.
His forearms' bull veins coarsed blue with metaphors marking
        my arrival.

Of course, students, I knew exactly who,
But being juicy,   nubile,   but not stupid, I
        professed indifference to his art.
He tried to charm me with a couplet,   and I yawned,
        told him to pass the wine glass,
Not his credentials before me like a search warrant stamped by
Pulitzer, National Book, and Pushcart.
Of course,   I knew,   students,   the great judges,
        had read all his winners, Swooned in the privacy of
        my room
Before sleuthing him down,   but undercover,
        apparently nonplused,

I pursed my lips,   licked them,   leaned in,
And asked,   *"Wouldn't you like to hear all you've missed,*
          snorting the dust off your shelves?"
He paused,   grunted,   nodded,   and
I unfurled adventures underwater,   staring barracuda in
          the beady eye,
The tense nights hugging gun slingers,   my arrest record,
          the war zones,
My tabletop tarantellas, but

Not one word,   students,   not a consonant of
          my budding verses,
The hours spent locked up with his pages taken me hostage,
My sestinas even then nestled between my thighs like whisky
          flasked beneath flapper skirts.
I knew,   students,   he had heard this tale before,
          handed out polite rejection slips,
The occasional apprenticeship beneath his pedestal,
Dusting the iambs between his hairy toes,
Then standing at attention in his boot camp while his rod
          pointed up,
Anticipating the lightning filled with
The electric verses with which he never deigned to power his
          female minions' work.

So,   students,   I feigned ignorance of all he practiced as
I straddled his moose torso and cooed enjambments

Like his muse moaning in surrender at last,   then left
abruptly,   smiling,
Demanding no return call,
Sauntering like a conqueror.

That way,   students,   a decade hence on his death bed,
His coma dreams conjured me,
Not his long-suffering mistress,
Her own scraps long squashed under the weight of all his
          papers,   her very desires
Alphabetized and
Dewey-decimaled in the midst of all his infidelities recorded in
          buoyant verses, not her,
His vanquished territory,   not the gaggle of yes-women,
But me.
That way,   students,   his last fantasy beckoned me
          like a lap dancer,
And finally,   released from the deafness of this world,
He understood my ruse,   recognized the practical joke
          played upon him,
The evening stolen,
The birthright snatched from Esau and all the rest
By me disguised,   who, like Jacob,   wrestled with
          the angels that one night,
And in tribute, students,   laughing,   he
          bequeathed his gift to me.

THE DAY I TAUGHT THE WIFE OF BATH TO WRITE

In this textual intervention, I
Am experienced, hence no *maydenhed*.
From that *auctoritee*, I pull out a
Wide chair for her to plop into, her

       Skirts hiked up and bodice ripped more than I
       Expected, but then, my newest student,
       By her own admission *hadde passed many*

       A straunge strem. My classroom was strangest
       Of all, no doubt, but it was time to ford
       Across this last divide. I handed her
       A pen.

       "You're so vivid, oh so vernacular!"
       I exclaimed, "but I got tired of your voice
       Authored only by a dead male poet.
       Don't let men author you. Let me help you.
       paint that lion for me, Miz Alysoun!"

She learned the alphabet, wrote her name.
She stared down at it like a cathedral

Spied afar after a long pilgrimage.
The gat-tooth grin faded. She wiped her eye.

> *"Sex hondred years have I goon wele far.*
> *Min ouen Jerusalem sits lokked within,*
> *And noght without. Experience is*
> *Swiche auctoritee, that have I sought*
>
> *"Min troth to plight, not to scriven*
> *For that alle clerkes men were,*
> *And min tale (and min tail),"* she winked,
> *"Have I put in gouvernance of Adam,*
>
> *"Though Eve wel useth hir instrument.*
> *And now have I maistrie of mannes'* stylus,
> *Also instrument of husbondes. I*
> *Write now min ouen propre parables,*

And ne more have ne nede of husbonde sex."

> I handed her a tissue. She wondered what it was.
> We debated all contraception,
> Lamented men no more wearing tights,
> But new words she learned to spell included
> "book," "rape," "battery," "pain,", and "wanderlust."
>
> She calls my bunker a *"cloistre,"* shakes her

Head in disgust. She crossed the Holy Land
During the black death, searching for herself.
She watches me cower in the basement.

She wants to know why I'm hiding in here
With all these hardbound dead men's expectations.
She calls me *"couard."* She wonders why I
Don't blowtorch the men's books insulting me.

After all, it's what she did years ago.
She got her hearing beaten out of her
Ear rejecting "expert" definitions.
She demands I leave this plague-tale cellar.

I try to explain censorship; despite
Her fictitiousness, she cannot be gagged.
Learning quickly new steps to the *olde daunce*,
Already proto-post-modern for years,

She asks me when last I saw "*brod dai-light.*"
Like characters by my neighbor Anne Rice,
I confess it years since I could see sunshine.
She exhorts me to periscope up top.

(I made mistakes, played her the title song
From *Cabaret.*) She wants two horses for
Us to ford the Mississippi West Bank

Over to the *Vieux Carré* for *"cok-tails"*—

A play on words that translates well, she thinks.
She plans to drink me under the table.

MACHIAVELLI AND SAINT THOMAS MOORE MANSPLAIN MY COUNTRY TO ME

The plague didn't vanish after the Late
Middle Ages, you know. Outbreaks popped up
In Tuscany and London then. Folks wrote.
I lean on the Saint Cuthbert Gospel and
Harley shelves. Niccolo and Thomas point
At me as if I were text and argue

In a Renaissance *dialogio* worthy
Of papal censure. They discuss me
As a thornless rose they pluck to prove their points.
"Her nation realizes rightly that
It needs a strong leader to make the State
Efficient," Niccolo whispers in rich

Middle Italian. Thomas Moore sneers like
A cat flicked with water on his whiskers.
He slaps the concrete wall and shouts Latin.
"Her State is based on a creed of ideals,
Of godly principles, unlike your book,"
The saint shouts, as silence implies consent.

Macchiavelli shouts back, *"But she is*
Resisting the inevitable! Men
Are greedy pigs. You know this, martire.
How much better for her to embrace it,
To rise with its tide! She could just blend in!"

Moore shakes his head again — *"One does not get*
To heaven on a feather bed. Thus is
Her America littered with martyrs.
She is resisting holy martyrdom,
I grant you, but preserves with us her soul.
We did not burn because she hid us here."

Niccolo scoffs, *"I will never burn, saint,*
Because I am the grandfather of all
Realists. Even Saddam Hussein, when
Captured in his basement spider hole, clutched
A copy of my book with his pistol—
I am eternal, while your bones are dust!"

I sigh. So does the woman next to me.
She is draped in blue silk, tall, braided hat
Pinned to her elegant head, eyebrows plucked
In the late medieval French Court, *très chic.*
She shares in Middle French. *"Anne, Three female*
Allegorical figures, each one wise,

"*Visit me in my library workspace*
In The Book of The City of Ladies.
They help me build a world where women run
The State. These chuckleheads," I translate her
Loosely, "*one of them was executed*
By his State. The other got banished. How
Can they presume they know something you don't?"
Christine de Pizan and I retreat to
My wine cellar and uncork a brilliant
Cognac while Moore and Machiavelli
Argue. We plan America without
Their help, their ends, their means, their principles,

Their warnings, their mirror texts to stare in
While changing nearly nothing, as men have.
When it is safe to climb out of this hole,
We'll use our lives as building blocks above.
We will host a tea dance for sanity,
Ladies of the city on the guest list.

WHEN THE SAINTS GO MARCHING

First at midnight, as Lisa and I had
Covenanted, a tennis ball plunged through
A bent pipe, clanging into a bucket.
That was the Paul Revere lantern for me.

At nine, a crash—a flurry of pounding
On the trap door above. I knew. I knew.
My hand got scraped by the giant wheel
I turned in a fury. For the first time

In an eon, I felt wind touch my hair.
It was so bright I felt motion sickness.
Lisa hugged me in a blanket like a
Spent marathoner at the finish line.

But she was the one who looked exhausted.
Where were my words? They were stashed in bookshelves
Still underground. I could not speak. Lisa
Handed me a glass as I bent limp and

Fetal, now barefoot on the hot sidewalk.
I heard bubbles as she poured. "Where are your shoes?"
She asked me. The dog remained below, still

Unsure it was safe to travel out. I blinked
In the big, blue air and called him to fetch
My flip-flops. He obeyed, his paws touching
Soil he could claw for the first time since we
Moved underground and hid the libraries.
"We won!" is all Lisa shouted, and I

Understood. "We won!" she repeated.
And then the rest of them arrived in stripes—
A brass band with magician assistants
From a show where the lady gets sawed

In half and put back together again.
"We won." I parroted in a whisper.
"We won," I repeated, white as a sheet.
The musicians started. Not knowing if

This were a Jazz funeral or just a
Second line, We danced. Lisa had brought a
Parasol. I staggered, then found the beat.
The dog circled us barking. We marched down

The avenue past buildings on fire, old
Men with long beards and torn clothes, past antique
Shops with broken panes but nothing stolen.
We marched past empty groceries and the

Occasional cadaver. We danced toward
City Hall, on Perdido Street—that word

Means "lost" in Creole—and we were tipsy
By then, staggering onto the steps.

I saw the flags I did not recognize,
But I recognized the song. It is ours.

Oh, how I long to be in that number!
We won. We won. We, the saints, went marching.

ACKNOWLEDGEMENTS

"At the Scuola di San Rocco" appeared in *Adelaide* in the United States and Portugal.

"How Things Have Gotten to This Point" appeared in *Ann Arbor Review*.

"The Letter Thorn" and "River Canto" appeared in *Backlash* in England.

"Bienvenue au Bunker," "December Bunker," "February Bunker," "January Bunker," and "March Bunker" appeared in *BlazeVox*.

"Buenos Aires 1952" appeared in *The Blend* in Australia.

"Woman Shot on Fontainebleau Drive" appeared in *Chronogram*.

"Blood or Milk" appeared in *Comstock Review* and was included in an art installation which projected poems on the walls of New Orleans buildings — *Voir Une Voie* by Swiss artist Manon Bellet.

"September Bunker" appeared in *Curator Magazine*.

"Before," "Findings at the Reichstag" appeared in *Ethos Literary Journal* in India.

"April Bunker," "May Bunker," and "July Bunker" appeared in *Foreign Literary Journal* in South Korea.

"The New Economy" appeared in *Hazmat Review*.

"From the Convent of Hefla" appeared in *Hidden City Quarterly*.

"Brunch with Lord Tennyson" appeared in *Illumen*.

"Norse Explorers Reach the Mississippi" appeared in *The Literary Bohemian.*

"A Confederacy of Objects" appeared in *Lou Lit Review.*

"The Saint" appeared in *New Song.*

"Where Louis, Lestat and I Bar-Crawl Bourbon Street" appeared in *One Art.*

"Outlaw Saints" appeared in *Oracle.*

"The Evening Stolen from the Great Poet" appeared in *Pacific Coast Journal.*

"Why" appeared in *Pemmican.*

"Dry Martinis at the National Arts Club" appeared in *The Pikeville Review.*

"Actual Nightmares I Had as a Toddler" appeared in *Quail Bell.*

"Altarpiece Diptych" appeared in *Qwerty* in Canada.

"August Bunker" appeared in *Red Rock Review.*

"Bunker Cuisine," "June Bunker," "Musical Newsreels," "My Face as a Damaged Manuscript," and "October Bunker" appeared in *Setu Bilingual Journal*

"Errands" appeared in *Shampoo.*

"My Afternoon with Laura Ingalls" appeared in *Silk Road Review.*

"Graveyard Shift" appeared in *Southampton Review.*

"Pajama Party with Gertrude Stein" appeared in *Vanilla.*

"Heather Lewis in September 1985" appeared in *Wild Violet.*

"To Sylvia Plath" appeared in *Willow.*

"Poem in Which I am a Reliquary, a Vierge Ouvrante" appeared in *The Women's Review of Books*

"About Hands" appeared in *Women and Gender Studies.*

About the Author

Anne Babson's first collection *The White Trash Pantheon* won the Colby H. Kullman prize from the Southern Writers Southern Writing Conference in Oxford, Mississippi. She wrote the libretto for the opera *Lotus Lives,* which has been performed in multiple cities and is slated for production once more in Montreal in 2018. She is the author of three chapbooks– *Poems Under Surveillance* is still in print with Finishing Line Press, and she has a forthcoming chapbook from Dancing Girl Press entitled *Dolly Shot.* She has been anthologized in the United States and in England, most recently in the notable collection *Nasty Women Poets: an Unapologetic Anthology of Subversive Verse* released in 2017. Her work has appeared in literary journals on five continents and has won numerous editorial awards. She has been nominated for the Pushcart Prize four times. She has received residency grants from Yaddo and Vermont Studio Center. Her blog about moving south, *The Carpetbaggers Journal,* has close to 50,000 hits and has been picked up by *Y'all Politics* and PBS-related websites. She writes lyrics for a variety of musical projects, most recently a blues album. She teaches writing and literature at Southeastern Louisiana University. She writes and lives in New Orleans.

ABOUT THE PRESS

Unsolicited Press was founded in 2012 and is based in Portland, Oregon. The small press publishes fiction, poetry, and creative nonfiction written by award-winning and emerging authors. Some of its authors include John W. Bateman, Anne Leigh Parrish, Adrian Ernesto Cepeda, and Raki Kopernik.

Learn more at www.unsolicitedpress.com

www.ingramcontent.com/pod-product-compliance
Lightning Source LLC
Chambersburg PA
CBHW030255070526
44654CB00045B/1042